Table of Contents

Introduction 3
  Benefits 4
Recipe 8
  Making Keto Zucchini Bread 8
  Mediavine 10
  90 Second Bread 11
  4-Ingredient Keto Almond Bread 12
  Keto Collagen Protein Bread 13
  Low-Carb Rye Bread 15
  Sourdough Keto Baguettes 18
Low-Carb Cauliflower Bread 20
  Keto Coconut Flour Bread 21
  The Best Low-Carb Garlic Bread 23
  Simple Keto Meatballs 25
  Garlic Cauliflower Breadsticks 26
  Keto Jalapeño Cheese Bread 30
  Keto Spinach Dip Stuffed Bread 31
  Pesto Pull-Apart Low Carb Bread 35
  Everything Keto Rolls 37
  4 Ingredient Low-Carb Cloud Bread 39
Cloud bread 41
  Cheesy Keto Hamburger Buns 42

- Parmesan & Tomato Keto Bread Buns 43
- Indian Fry Bread Recipe (Low Carb) 46
- Keto Low Carb Banana Bread Recipe With Almond Flour - Sugar Free 48
- Blueberry Crumb Loaf – Keto/Low Carb/Gluten Free 50
- Keto Lemon Bread With Poppy Seed 52
- Low Carb Lemon Blueberry Zucchini Bread Recipe With Almond Flour 54
- Zucchini Coconut Bread 56
- Low-Carb Lemon Blueberry Bread 58
- Keto Gingerbread Cake 59
- Delicious gingerbread loaf 62
- Keto Pumpkin Bread 64
- Low Carb Focaccia Bread 67
- Lemon & Rosemary Low Carb Shortbread 69
- Low Carb Microwave Hamburger Bun 72
- Bacon Breakfast Bagels 73
- Keto Breadsticks 76
- Jalapeno Cornbread Mini Loaves 79
- 90-Second Keto Bread 81

Introduction

An Introduction to Keto bread that fully explains the principles of the diet and shows you exactly how to achieve your health and weight loss goals without sacrificing the baked goods you love. The Basics of Home Baking with easy to follow instructions, tips, and tricks for baking amazing keto-friendly recipes at home Amazing Ketogenic Baking Recipes that your family will rave about including loaves, breadsticks, buns, pretzels, muffins, cakes, and snacksNutritional Information for Every Recipe so you can easily track exactly what you are consumingSay goodbye to the sacrifice of sticking to your Keto bread with Sabrina Asmara's Keto Bread Cookbook, your go-to resource for making the Ketogenic Diet a complete lifestyle. The book begins with an incredibly rudimentary introduction to KETO, including a few variations of the diet along with some statements most following a KETO bread wouldn't agree with such as "there's no set rule for carb intake", and assumptions including "the ketogenic bread process is successful in approximately 90% of its users" Enjoy good health and rapid fat loss on the Ketogenic bread without giving up the baked goods you love Humble, honest home cooking to help you stay on the ketogenic bread does not have to mean sacrificing the foods you loved most. With the goal of making keto accessible and convenient for everyone, keto baker Sabrina Asmara brings her passion for delicious, healthy low-carb baking recipes to your kitchen. The Keto Bread Cookbook is the first choice for Keto dieters who want to have it all, including all of their favorite sandwiches, burgers, loaves, breadsticks, buns, pretzels, muffins, cakes, and snacks, all easily made at home in your own kitchen with no special appliances or hard-to-find exotic ingredients. The ultimate Keto Baker's Cookbook for ketogenic baking recipes.

Benefits

No need to give up bread on keto. This keto-friendly bread has a number of health benefits thanks to the good-for-you ingredients.

Pastured Eggs for a Better Brain

Did you know that even paleo and gluten-free bread can spike your blood sugar and lead to a massive energy crash, That's because most of the bread you find on grocery store shelves is high in carbohydrates and low in brain-boosting fats. They certainly have no place in a low-carb diet.

Instead, you'll make this super easy keto bread with almond flour, coconut flour, and pastured eggs all ingredients that will keep your blood sugar steady and help banish brain fog. Eggs are well-known for their protein content, but that's not their only claim to fame. In fact, eggs are a powerhouse of nutrition when it comes to brain food. They are a great source of choline, an essential nutrient for brain function and development. Choline also supports focus and learning, making it a crucial compound for cognitive performance, no matter your age. But that's not all eggs are also rich in a variety of B vitamins, including folate, biotin, riboflavin, pantothenic acid, and B12. B vitamins are crucial for brain health and development throughout your life. Research indicates a link between B12 deficiency and cognitive impairment in the elderly. You can help slow down brain aging with more B vitamin-rich foods like eggs. Speaking of keeping your brain young, another ingredient in many keto recipes is vitamin E-rich almond flour. Vitamin E is a powerful antioxidant that is being studied for its beneficial effects on cognition in people with Alzheimer's disease.

Nutrients for Better Eye Health

Digital devices, artificial lighting, and even the sun your eyes are constantly challenged. Although these sources of blue light may seem unavoidable, there's hope yet. Lutein and zeaxanthin are phytochemicals that give fruits and vegetables their yellow and orange hues. You can also find them in abundance in egg yolks. Lutein and zeaxanthin act as powerful antioxidants that help protect your body against free radicals. Too many free radicals can trigger cell damage that leads to diseases like cancer and age-related cognitive decline. But lutein and zeaxanthin are especially good for your eyes. Not only do they protect your eyes from light damage by filtering blue light, but they also can help protect from age-related eye diseases like macular degeneration and cataracts. Eggs are also incredibly bioavailable, so you won't just get a decent dose of antioxidants, you'll get a dose that your body can absorb and use. Consuming one egg a day raises your levels of lutein and zeaxanthin. And that's just one component of 90-second bread.

A Stronger Immune System

If you're constantly tired or always coming down with a cold, your immune system might need a boost. Luckily, you don't have to spend hundreds of dollars on supplements when you've got nutrient-dense foods at the ready. Coconut is one of the best foods for immune health. Coconut oil in particular is known for battling dangerous bacteria and for its anti-inflammatory effects. Coconut is also rich in medium chain triglycerides (MCTs), which are being studied for potential cancer-fighting properties. Almonds are another immune-boosting food thanks to their manganese content. Manganese supports the production of a powerful antioxidant called SOD (superoxide dismutase) that protects the energy production centers in your cells, aka mitochondria. Mitochondria help turn the food you eat into energy your body uses to function. When your mitochondria aren't working optimally, you'll be tired, slow, and less likely to fight off viruses and bugs. The vitamin E in almonds has also been shown to support immune health, especially in the elderly. This potent antioxidant works to protect and increase communication between your cells, and boost immune health by fighting off bacteria and viruses. Almond flour is also an excellent source of dietary fiber, protein, and monounsaturated fats while being low in carbohydrates. Not bad for a piece of keto almond flour bread. This low-carb bread recipe is bound to be a hit in your household and will certainly become your go-to option when you're craving a BLT. Use it for your favorite eggy breakfast sandwich, drizzle it with olive oil and sea salt, or make a quick batch before heading to work in the morning. Just pop it in the toaster and add your favorite cheddar or cream cheese on top. Or perhaps, try it out with this mouth-watering avocado pesto sauce. It will easily become one of your favorite low-carb recipes.

Recipe

Making Keto Zucchini Bread
Ingredients

- 3 ounces (1 cup) of Almond Flour

- 2 ounces (½ cup) of Coconut Flour

- 1 teaspoon of Salt

- ½ teaspoon of Pepper

- 2 teaspoons of Baking Powder

- 1 teaspoon of Xanthan Gum

- 5 Eggs

- ⅔ cup of Butter, melted

- 4 ounces (1 cup) Of Cheddar Cheese, grated

- 6 ounces (1 cup) of Zucchini, grated and liquid squeezed out

- 6 ounces (1 cup) of Bacon, diced

How To Make Keto Zucchini Bread

- Preheat oven to 175C/350F.

- In a large bowl add the almond flour, coconut flour, salt, pepper, baking powder and xanthan gum. Mix well.

- Add the eggs and melted butter and mix well.

- Fold through ¾ of the cheddar, along with the zucchini and bacon.

- Spoon into your greased 9in ceramic loaf dish (if using a metal dish, line with parchment paper) and bake for 35 minutes, remove from the oven and top with the remaining cheese.

- Bake for another 10-15 minutes, until the cheese has browned and a skewer comes out clean.

- Leave to cool for 20 minutes.

- Slice into 12 slices and enjoy warm.

Mediavine
Ingredients

- 3 ounces almond flour

- 2 ounces coconut flour

- 1/2 teaspoon salt

- 1/2 teaspoon pepper

- 2 teaspoons baking powder

- 1 teaspoon xanthan gum

- 5 large eggs

- 2/3 cup butter melted

- 4 ounces cheddar cheese grated

- 6 ounces zucchini grated and liquid squeezed out

- 6 ounces bacon diced

Instructions

• Preheat oven to 175C/350F.

• In a large bowl add the almond flour, coconut flour, salt, pepper, baking powder and xanthan gum. Mix well.

• Add the eggs and melted butter and mix well.

• Fold through ¾ of the cheddar, along with the zucchini and bacon.

• Spoon into your greased 9in ceramic loaf dish (if using a meat dish, line with parchment paper) and bake for 35 minutes, remove from the oven and top with the remaining cheese.

• Bake for another 10-15 minutes, until the cheese has browned and a skewer comes out clean.

• Leave to cool for 20 minutes.

• Slice into 12 slices and enjoy warm.

90 Second Bread
Ingredients

• 2 tablespoons almond flour

- 1/2 tablespoon coconut flour

- 1/4 teaspoon baking powder

- 1 egg

- 1/2 tablespoon melted butter or ghee

- 1 tablespoon unsweetened milk of choice

Instructions

- Mix all ingredients in a small bowl and whisk until smooth.

- Grease a 3×3-inch glass microwave-safe bowl or mold with butter, ghee, or coconut oil.

- Pour your mixture into your well-greased bowl or mold and microwave on high for 90 seconds.

- Carefully remove your bread from the glass dish or mold.

- Slice, toast, and melt butter on top, if desired.

4-Ingredient Keto Almond Bread

Ingredients

- ½ cup butter

- 2 Tbsp coconut oil

- 7 eggs

- 2 cups almond flour

Instructions

- Preheat the oven to 355°F.

- Line a loaf pan with parchment paper.

- Mix the eggs in a bowl on high for up to two minutes.

- Add the almond flour, melted coconut oil and melted butter to the eggs. Continue to mix.

- Scrape the mix into the loaf pan.

- Bake for 45-50 minutes or until a toothpick comes out clean.

Keto Collagen Protein Bread

Ingredients

- 1/2 cup Perfect Keto Collagen (about 50g)

- 5 egg whites and yolks separated

- 6 tbsp coconut flour

- 3 tbsp coconut milk full-fat

- 1 tsp xanthan gum

- 1 tsp baking powder keto friendly

- 1 pinch sea salt

- 1 tbsp coconut oil melted (+ more for greasing)

Instructions

- Preheat the oven to 325 F.

- In a bowl, combine all the dry ingredients.

- In a small bowl, whisk together coconut milk, egg yolks, and melted coconut oil.

- In another bowl, whip egg whites until peaks form.

- Fold both dry and wet ingredients in the whipped egg whites bowl and mix until incorporated.

- Brush your loaf dish (9x5x3-inch size) with coconut oil.

- Pour the batter into a loaf dish and bake for 40 minutes.

- Let cool completely and slice.

Low-Carb Rye Bread

Dry Ingredients:

- 2 packed cups flax meal (300 g/ 10.6 oz)

- 1 cup coconut flour (120 g/ 4.2 oz)

- 2 tbsp caraway seeds (or rosemary)

- 1 tbsp + 1 tsp baking powder

- 1 tbsp Erythritol or Swerve (10 g/ 0.4 oz) or 3-5 drops liquid stevia

- 1/4 cup ground chia seeds (32 g/ 1.1 oz) or 1 tsp xanthan gum

- 1 tsp salt or more to taste (pink Himalayan rock salt)

Wet Ingredients:

- 8 eggs, separated

- 1/2 cup softened but not melted ghee, butter or 1/2 cup extra virgin olive oil (110 g/ 3.9 oz)

- 2 tbsp toasted sesame oil

- 1/3 cup apple cider vinegar (80 ml/ 2.7 fl oz)

- 1 cup warm water (240 ml/ 8 fl oz)

Instructions

• Move the oven rack to the centre position of the oven, and preheat to 190 °C/ 375 °F (conventional), or 170 °C/ 340 °F (fan assisted). Add the dry ingredients to a large bowl and thoroughly whisk to combine (ground flaxseed, coconut flour, caraway, baking soda, Erythritol, salt and xanthan gum or ground chia seeds). It is especially important to evenly distribute the xanthan gum (or ground chia seeds).Low-Carb Rye Bread

• Separate the egg yolks from the egg whites and keep the egg whites aside. Add softened ghee or butter and toasted sesame oil into the eggs yolks. (Note: Although the original recipe doesn't ask for separating the eggs, I found that doing so makes the bread fluffier.)Low-Carb Rye Bread

• Cream the egg yolks and the ghee (butter or olive oil) until smooth. In a separate bowl, whisk the egg whites with cream of tartar until they create soft peaks.Low-Carb Rye Bread

• Add the dry mixture to the bowl with the egg yolk mixture and process well. It's a thick batter, and will come together slowly. Take the time to make sure everything is thoroughly mixed.Low-Carb Rye Bread

• Add the vinegar and mix in well.Low-Carb Rye Bread

• Add warm water and process until combined.Low-Carb Rye Bread

• Add the egg whites and gently fold them in. Try not to deflate the batter completely.Low-Carb Rye Bread

• Grease a large loaf pan with some ghee or butter and add the batter. Smooth the batter out evenly in the pan and "cut" it on top using a spatula to create a wave effect. If you use a silicon loaf pan, you won't need to grease it.Low-Carb Rye Bread

• Bake for approximately 50-60 minutes (depends on the oven). When the bread is ready, remove from loaf pan to a cooling rack, and allow to cool thoroughly.Low-Carb Rye Bread

• Slice thinly and enjoy!Low-Carb Rye Bread

• It makes great toast under the broiler and it's delicious in sandwiches, panini, with grass-fed butter or cream cheese and as a dipping bread with extra virgin olive oil.

Sourdough Keto Baguettes

Dry ingredients:

- 1 1/2 cup almond flour (150 g/ 5.3 oz)

- 2/3 cup psyllium husks - will be powdered, will make about 1/3 cup psyllium husk powder (40 g/ 1.4 oz)

- 1/2 cup coconut flour (60 g/ 2.1 oz)

- 1/2 packed cup flax meal (75 g/ 2.6 oz)

- 1 tsp baking soda

- 1 tsp sea salt

Wet Ingredients:

- 6 large egg whites

- 2 large eggs

- 3/4 cup low-fat buttermilk (180 g/ 6.5 oz) - full-fat would make them too heavy and they may not rise

- 1/4 cup white wine vinegar or apple cider vinegar (60 ml/ 2 fl oz)

- 1 cup lukewarm water (240 ml/ 8 fl oz)

Instructions

- Preheat the oven to 180 °C/ 355 °F (fan assisted), or 200 °C/ 400 °F (conventional). Use a kitchen scale to measure all the ingredients carefully. Mix all the dry ingredients in a bowl (almond flour, coconut flour, ground flaxseed, psyllium powder, baking soda, and salt).

- Sourdough Keto Baguettes

- In a separate bowl, mix the eggs, egg whites and buttermilk.

- Sourdough Keto Baguettes

- Add the egg mixture and process well using a mixer until the dough is thick. Add vinegar and lukewarm water and process until well combined.

- Sourdough Keto Baguettes

- Do not over-process the dough. Using a spoon, make 8 regular or 16 mini baguettes and place them on a baking tray lined with parchment paper or a non-stick mat. They will rise, so make sure to leave some space between them. Optionally, score the baguettes diagonally and make 3-4 cuts.Sourdough Keto Baguettes

- Place in the oven and cook for 10 minutes. Then, reduce the temperature to 150 °C/ 300 °F (fan assisted), or 170 °C/ 340 °F (conventional) and bake for another 30-45 minutes (small baguettes will take less time to cook).Sourdough Keto Baguettes

- Remove from the oven, let the tray cool down and place the baguettes on a rack to cool down to room temperature. Store them at room temperature if you plan to use them in the next couple of days or store in the freezer for up to 3 months.

- Sourdough Keto Baguettes

- Enjoy just like regular baguettes! To save time, mix all the dry ingredients ahead and store in a zip-lock bag and add a label with the number of servings. When ready to be baked, just add the wet ingredients.

Low-Carb Cauliflower Bread
Ingredients

- 2 cups almond flour

- 5 eggs

- ¼ cup psyllium husk

- 1 cup cauliflower rice

Instructions

- Preheat oven to 350 °F.

- Line a loaf pan with parchment paper or coconut oil cooking spray. Set aside.

- In a large bowl or food processor, mix the almond flour and psyllium husk.

- Beat in the eggs on high for up to two minutes.

- Mix in the cauliflower rice and blend well.

- Pour the cauliflower mixture into the loaf pan.

- Bake for up to 55 minutes.

Keto Coconut Flour Bread

Ingredients

- 1/2 cup Coconut flour

- 1 stick butter (8 tbsp)

- 6 large eggs

- 1 tsp Baking powder
- 2 tsp Dried Rosemary
- 1/2-1 tsp garlic powder
- 1/2 tsp Onion powder
- 1/4 tsp Pink Himalayan Salt

Instructions

- Combine dry ingredients (coconut flour, baking powder, onion, garlic, rosemary and salt) in a bowl and set aside.
- Add 6 eggs to a separate bowl and beat with a hand mixer until you get see bubbles at the top.
- Melt the stick of butter in the microwave and slowly add it to the eggs as you beat with the hand mixer.
- Once wet and dry ingredients are fully combined in separate bowls, slowly add the dry ingredients to the wet ingredients as you mix with the hand mixture.
- Grease an 8x4 loaf pan and pour the mixture into it evenly.

- Bake at 350 for 40-50 minutes (time will vary depending on your oven).

- Let it rest for 10 minutes before removing from the pan. Slice up and enjoy with butter or toasted.

The Best Low-Carb Garlic Bread
Ingredients

- 1 recipe Sourdough Keto Baguettes, 8 regular or 16 small baguettes

- Garlic & Herb Compound Butter:

- 1/2 cup softened unsalted butter (113 g/ 4 oz)

- 1/2 tsp salt (I like pink Himalayan salt)

- 1/4 tsp ground black pepper

- 2 tbsp extra virgin olive oil (30 ml)

- 4 cloves garlic, crushed

- 2 tbsp freshly chopped parsley or 2 tsp dried parsley

- Topping:

- 1/2 cup grated Parmesan cheese (45 g/ 1.6 oz)

- 2 tbsp fresh parsley

Optional: drizzle with extra virgin olive oil

Instructions

- Prepare the keto sourdough baguettes by following this recipe (you can make 8 regular or 16 mini baguettes).The Best Low-Carb Garlic Bread

- Prepare the garlic butter (or any other flavoured butter). Make sure all the ingredients have reached room temperature before mixing them in a medium bowl.The Best Low-Carb Garlic Bread

- Cut the baked baguettes in half and spread the flavoured butter on top of each half (1-2 teaspoons per piece).The Best Low-Carb Garlic Bread

- Sprinkle with grated Parmesan and place back in the oven to crisp up for a few more minutes.The Best Low-Carb Garlic Bread

- When done, remove from the oven. Optionally, drizzle with some olive oil and serve while still warm.

Simple Keto Meatballs

Ingredients

- 1 lb. ground beef
- 1 large egg
- 1/2 cup grated parmesan
- 1/2 cup shredded mozzarella
- 1 tbsp minced garlic
- 1 tsp black pepper
- 1/2 tsp salt

Instructions

- Preheat oven to 400 degrees. Line baking sheet with parchment paper.
- In a mixing bowl, using hands, combine all ingredients and knead together until well-incorporated.
- Form mixture into equal-sized meatballs and place on prepared baking sheet.
- Bake for 18-20 minutes.
- Allow to cool slightly and serve warm.

Garlic Cauliflower Breadsticks

Ingredients

- 2 cups riced cauliflower
- 1 tbsp organic butter
- 3 tsp minced garlic
- 1/4 tsp crushed red pepper flakes
- 1/2 tsp italian seasoning
- 1/8 tsp kosher salt
- 1 cup shredded mozzarella cheese
- 1 egg
- Grated parmesan cheese (the powder kind)

Instructions

- Preheat your oven to 350 degrees F.
- Next, assuming you have already riced a head of cauliflower and measured your two cups, microwave for three minutes. riced cauliflower

- Next, melt butter in a small skillet over low heat. Add garlic and red pepper flakes to butter and cook over low heat for two to three minutes (don't let the butter brown!)

- Add the butter and garlic mixture to the bowl of cooked cauliflower. Add Italian seasoning and salt to the bowl. Mix.

- Refrigerate for 10 minutes (don't want to cook the egg now do you?).

- Add the egg and mozzarella cheese to your bowl. Mix.

- Cut a layer of parchment paper to fill the bottom of a 9×9 baking dish and grease up with some butter or your cooking spray of choice (you never can be too careful with these cauliflower recipes!)

- Add to your dish and smooth into a thin layer using your hands. Garlic Cauliflower Breadsticks

- Bake for 30 minutes. After 30 minutes, take out of the oven, top with some more mozzarella cheese and a few shakes of some powdered parmesan as you like.

- Cook for an additional 8 minutes, then remove from oven and slice into strips. Serve with your favorite low-sugar/carb tomato sauce. Mine only has 2g of carbs for a whole half cup!

Garlic Cauliflower Breadsticks

Ingredients

- 2 cups riced cauliflower

- 1 tbsp organic butter

- 3 tsp minced garlic

- 1/4 tsp crushed red pepper flakes

- 1/2 tsp italian seasoning

- 1/8 tsp kosher salt

- 1 cup shredded mozzarella cheese

- 1 egg

- Grated parmesan cheese (the powder kind)

Instructions

- Preheat your oven to 350 degrees F.

- Next, assuming you have already riced a head of cauliflower and measured your two cups, microwave for three minutes.

- Next, melt butter in a small skillet over low heat. Add garlic and red pepper flakes to butter and cook over low heat for two to three minutes (don't let the butter brown!)

- Add the butter and garlic mixture to the bowl of cooked cauliflower. Add Italian seasoning and salt to the bowl. Mix.

- Refrigerate for 10 minutes (don't want to cook the egg now do you?).

- Add the egg and mozzarella cheese to your bowl. Mix.

- Cut a layer of parchment paper to fill the bottom of a 9×9 baking dish and grease up with some butter or your cooking spray of choice (you never can be too careful with these cauliflower recipes!)

- Add to your pan and smooth into a thin layer with using your palms.

- Bake for 30 minutes. After 30 minutes, take out of the oven, top with some more mozzarella cheese and a few shakes of some powdered parmesan as you like.

- Cook for an additional 8 minutes, then remove from oven and slice into strips. Serve with your favorite low-sugar/carb tomato sauce. Mine only has 2g of carbs for a whole half cup.

Keto Jalapeño Cheese Bread
Ingredients

- 4 large eggs

- 2 heaped tbsp full-fat greek yogurt (60 g/ 2.1 oz)

- 1/3 cup coconut flour (40 g/ 1.4 oz)

- 2 tbsp whole psyllium husks (8 g/ 0.3 oz)

- 1/2 tsp sea salt

- 1 tsp gluten-free baking powder

- 1/2 cup shredded sharp cheddar cheese, divided (57 g/ 2 oz)

- 1/4 cup diced pickled jalapeños (28 g/ 1 oz)

- Few sliced jalapeños for topping (14 g/ 0.5 oz)

Instructions

- Preheat the oven to 190 °C/ 375 °F (conventional), or 170 °C/ 340 °F (fan assisted) and line a baking sheet with parchment paper. In a medium bowl whisk together the eggs and Greek yogurt.

- Add coconut flour, psyllium husks, salt and baking powder.Keto Jalapeño Cheese Bread

- Once smooth stir in half of the shredded cheddar cheese.Keto Jalapeño Cheese Bread

- Add the diced jalapeños.Keto Jalapeño Cheese Bread

- Press the dough into a 2.5 cm/ 1 inch thick sphere on the baking sheet. Top with remaining cheese and additional jalapeños if desired.Keto Jalapeño Cheese Bread

- Bake for 15 minutes or until golden and fluffy. Cut into 8 squares.Keto Jalapeño Cheese Bread

- Serve warm or let it cool down.

Keto Spinach Dip Stuffed Bread
Ingredients

- "Bread" Dough
- 5 ounces shredded mozzarella
- 1 ounce shredded cheddar
- 1 ounce cream cheese
- 1 tablespoon butter
- 1/2 teaspoon Italian seasoning
- 1/2 teaspoon garlic powder
- 1/2 cup + 2 tablespoons blanched almond flour
- 1 tablespoon oat fiber
- 1/2 teaspoon xantham gum
- 1 teaspoon baking powder
- 1 teaspoon active dry yeast
- 2 tablespoons warm (~110F) water, for dissolving yeast
- 2 large eggs (one for dough, one for egg wash)
- 1 tablespoon coconut (or almond) flour, for kneading dough

Filling

- 1 1/2 cups keto spinach dip

- 1 ounce shredded cheddar or mozzarella

- 2 tablespoons grated parmesan

Instructions

- Preheat oven to 375F. Prepare 9" round baking pan by thoroughly greasing, or a baking sheet by lining with parchment paper (see above).

- Add yeast to warm water and allow to dissolve, stirring to break up any clumps.

- Sift together dry ingredients (almond flour, oat fiber, xantham gum, baking powder, garlic powder, Italian seasoning).

- In a microwave-safe bowl, combine shredded cheeses, cream cheese, and butter. Microwave for 60-90 seconds, or until cheese is melted. Stir to combine.

- Add dry ingredients, one egg, and yeast mixture to melted cheese mixture and mix well until dough forms a ball. Turn dough onto a flat surface sprinkled with the coconut flour and knead gently, 15-20 times or until no longer "sticky" to the touch.

• Optional: For best results, cover the dough with a damp cloth and allow to rise in a warm place for 10-15 minutes.

• Divide dough into two approximately equal sections, and roll each into a ~9" circle.

• Spread the spinach dip on one circle of dough, stopping just before the edges. Top with shredded cheese and parmesan. Layer the other circle of dough on top of the filling.

• Make 12 slices (like cutting a pizza) through both layers of dough, being careful to leave them connected in the center. Pick up each "slice" and twist gently so that the "bottom" layer of dough is on top.

• Beat the remaining egg and evenly brush the the exposed dough with the egg wash.

• Bake in the preheated oven for about 25 minutes, or until golden brown. Optionally, brush with melted garlic butter before serving.

- Best served warm. Store refrigerated for up to 5 days. Reheat in the microwave or in the oven at a low (~250F) temperature.

Pesto Pull-Apart Low Carb Bread
Ingredients

- 1 recipe Sourdough Keto Baguettes

- 2/3 cup pesto, you can make your own pesto (170 g/ 6 oz)

- 1/2 cup grated Parmesan or other Italian hard cheese (45 g/ 1.6 oz)

Basil & Arugula Pesto:

- 1/2 cup walnuts or pecans (50 g/ 1.8 oz)

- 1 bunch fresh basil (28 g/ 1 oz)

- 2 cups arugula (20 g/ 0.7 oz)

- 4 cloves garlic, sliced

- 2 tsp lemon zest

- 1 tbsp lemon juice (15 ml)

- 1/4 cup extra virgin olive oil

- Sea salt and pepper, to taste

Instructions

- Preheat the oven to 170 °C/ 325 °F (conventional oven), or 150 °C/ 300 °F (fan assisted oven).

- To make pesto, place all of the ingredients except olive oil in a food processor. Blend until smooth. You'll need just 2/3 cup of the pesto (or use more or less to taste). Any leftover pesto can be stored in the fridge and used in zucchini noodles and other keto recipes.Pesto Pull-Apart Low Carb Bread

- Prepare the bread dough by following this recipe. Form the dough into rolls (I made 12) but you could easily make 9 bigger ones if you prefer.

- Spoon roughly 1 tbsp of pesto into the centre of each bread roll and work it into the dough with your hands. Roll back into balls.Pesto Pull-Apart Low Carb Bread

- Grease an oven proof skillet with a little coconut oil or butter to prevent sticking.

- Arrange the rolls in a circular pattern to roughly cover the base of the pan. They will expand on cooking.

- Sprinkle with Parmesan. I didn't include the Parmesan in the pesto as I wanted more on top.

- Pesto Pull-Apart Low Carb Bread

- Bake for 50 to 60 minutes or until golden and cooked through. When done, remove from the oven and let the bread cool down for 5 minutes.

- Pesto Pull-Apart Low Carb BreadTo prevent the bread from getting moist transfer from the skillet to a cooling wrack.Pesto Pull-Apart Low Carb BreadTastes best when served warm. Once cooled can be stored in the fridge for up to 3 days, or freeze for up to 3 months.

- Pesto Pull-Apart Low Carb Bread

Everything Keto Rolls
Ingredients

- 120 grams of sunflower seed flour

- 5 tablespoons of ground psyllium husk

- 2 tsp baking powder

- 1/2 tsp salt

- 1 and 1/4th cup boiling water

- 2 tsp apple cider vinegar

- 1 tablespoon everything but the bagel seasoning + 1 tablespoon for the tops

- 3 Egg whites- I used organic ones from a carton so I don't have to find a use for the yokes. If you use whites from the carton its 6 tablespoons.

- Grated cheese for the tops is optional

Instructions

- Pre-heat oven to 350 and line a baking sheet with parchment

- Mix your sunflower seed flour, ground psyllium husk, baking powder, salt and seasoning in a bowl and whisk until combined

- Add the boiling water and mix for about a minute. You may need to switch to a spatula or wooden spoon instead of a whisk now.

- Add the apple cider vinegar and mix again.

- Finally when the mix has cooled a bit add the egg whites to the bowl. The mix will be well formed and it may seem that the eggs whites won't incorporate- just keep mixing and folding. Kneed the dough with greased hands until everything is incorporated. It won't take long.

• With greased hands form 6 balls. The dough is fairly loose and slightly sticky but you can still make balls.

• Sprinkle your seasoning over the top and press it in so it sticks.

• Cook in the oven for 45 min- remove from oven and top with cheese if desired and then bake the remaining 15 minutes.

• Let fully cool before cutting open!

• Store in an airtight container in the fridge.

4 Ingredient Low-Carb Cloud Bread
Ingredients

• 3 eggs, room temperature

• 3 tbsp cream cheese, softened

• 1/4 tsp cream of tartar

• 1/4 tsp salt

Instructions

• Preheat oven to 300°F and line two baking sheets with parchment paper.

• Carefully separate egg whites from yolks. Place whites in one bowl and yolks in another.

• In the bowl of egg yolks, add cream cheese and mix together with a hand mixer until well-combined.

• In the bowl of egg whites, add cream of tartar and salt. Using a hand mixer, mix together at high speed until stiff peaks form.

• Pouring slowly, use a spatula or spoon to add yolk mixture to egg whites and carefully fold in until there are no white streaks.

• Spoon mixture onto prepared baking sheet about ½ to ¾ inches tall and about 5 inches apart.

• Bake in the oven on middle rack for 30 minutes, until tops are lightly golden brown.

• Allow to cool (they will likely be too crumbly directly out of the oven) and enjoy.

Cloud bread

Ingredients

- 2 Eggs
- 75g Cream Cheese (softened)
- 1 tsp Ground Psyllium Husks
- 1/2 tsp Baking Powder
- 1/2 tsp Cream of Tartar
- Salt
- Seeds or herbs for topping (optional)

Instructions

- Preheat oven to 160c/320f
- Line a baking tray with baking paper
- Seperate the eggs, and place the yolks in one bowl and the whites in another
- Whisk the egg whites with the cream of tartar and a pinch of salt until they form stiff peaks, set aside
- In the other bowl beat the egg yolks and cream cheese until combined

- Add the psyllium husk powder and baking powder to the cream cheese mixture and stir to combine

- Fold the egg whites into the into the cream cheese mixture gently to try to keep it light and airy

- Divide the mixture into round 4 piles on the baking tray

- Sprinkle with any seeds or herbs if you like

- Bake for 20-25 minutes until they are golden brown

Cheesy Keto Hamburger Buns
Ingredients

- 2 cups mozzarella cheese (shredded)

- 4 oz. cream cheese

- 4 large eggs

- 3 cups almond flour

- 4 tbsp. melted grass-fed butter

- Sesame seeds

Instructions

- Preheat oven to 400°F.

- Line a baking sheet with parchment paper.

- In a large bowl, combine mozzarella and cream cheese. Heat in the microwave for 10 seconds, or until both cheeses are melted.

- Add 3 eggs to your cheese mixture, and stir to combine. Add your almond flour, then stir again.

- Form dough into 6 bun-shaped balls then place on prepared baking sheet.

- Whisk your last egg. Brush each dough ball with melted butter and your whisked egg, then sprinkle with sesame seeds.

- Bake until golden, about 10-12 minutes.

Parmesan & Tomato Keto Bread Buns
Dry ingredients

- 3/4 cup almond flour (75 g/ 2.7 oz)

- 2 1/2 tbsp psyllium husk powder (20 g/ 0.7 oz)

- 1/4 cup coconut flour (30 g/ 1.1 oz)

- 1/4 cup packed cup flax meal (38 g/ 1.3 oz)

- 1 tsp cream of tartar or apple cider vinegar
- 1/2 tsp baking soda
- 2/3 cup grated Parmesan cheese or other Italian hard cheese (60 g/ 2.1 oz)
- 1/3 cup chopped sun-dried tomatoes (37 g/ 1.3 oz)
- 1/4 - 1/2 tsp pink sea salt
- 2 tbsp sesame seeds (18 g/ 0.6 oz) - or use 2 tbsp sunflower, flax, poppy seeds, or 1 tbsp caraway seeds

Wet ingredients

- 3 large egg whites
- 1 large egg
- 1 cups boiling water (240 ml/ 8 fl oz)

Instructions

- Preheat the oven to 175 °C/ 350 °F (fan assisted). Use a kitchen scale to measure all the ingredients and add them to a mixing bowl (apart from the sesame seeds which are used for topping): almond flour, coconut flour, flax meal, psyllium husk powder, cream of tartar, baking soda, salt, parmesan cheese and sun dried tomatoes. Mix all the dry ingredients together.Parmesan & Tomato Keto Bread Buns

• Add the egg whites and eggs and process well using a mixer until the dough is thick.

• The reason you shouldn't use only whole eggs is that the buns wouldn't rise with so many egg yolks in. Don't waste them - use them for making Home-made Mayo, Easy Hollandaise Sauce or Lemon Curd.Parmesan & Tomato Keto Bread Buns

• Add boiling water and process until well combined.Parmesan & Tomato Keto Bread Buns

• Using a spoon, divide the keto buns mix into 5 and roll into buns using your hands. Place them on a non-stick baking tray or on parchment paper. They will grow in size, so make sure to leave some space between them. You can even use small tart trays.

• Top each of the buns with sesame seeds (or any other seeds) and gently press them into the dough, so they don't fall out. Place in the oven and cook for about 45 - 50 minutes until golden on top.Parmesan & Tomato Keto Bread Buns

- Remove from the oven, let the tray cool down and place the buns on a rack to cool to room temperature.Parmesan & Tomato Keto Bread Buns

- Enjoy just like you would regular bread — with butter, ham or cheese!Parmesan & Tomato Keto Bread BunsStore in a tupperware for 2-3 days or freeze for up to 3 months.

Indian Fry Bread Recipe (Low Carb)
Ingredients

- 1 ½ Cups Shredded Mozzarella Cheese

- 2 Tablespoons Cream Cheese

- 1 Egg

- 1 Teaspoon Baking Powder

- 1 Cup Almond Flour (or you can use Trim Healthy Mama Baking Blend)

- 1 ½ Cups Refined Coconut Oil (for frying)

Instructions

- Heat coconut oil in a frying pan over medium-low heat.

Make the Dough:

- In a large microwaveable bowl, melt mozzarella cheese and cream cheese.

- Stir will, then add egg and baking powder and stir again.

- Add almond flour, 1/4 cup at a time, stirring well after each addition. (You should have an even, homogenous dough. You may have to knead it with your hands a bit.)

- Turn dough onto parchment paper and divide into four balls.

- Flatten each ball between parchment paper and roll into a 6-8 inch circle with a rolling pin.

Fry the Dough:

When the oil has heated, fry dough (one at a time) for about 20 seconds, then flip and fry 20 seconds on the other side. The bread should be a light golden brown color.

Remove from oil and drain on paper towels.

Serve with all your favorite taco toppings for an Indian Fry Bread Taco.

Keto Low Carb Banana Bread Recipe With Almond Flour - Sugar Free

Ingredients

- 2 cup Blanched almond flour

- 1/4 cup Coconut flour

- 1/2 cup Walnuts (chopped; plus more for topping if desired)

- 2 tsp Gluten-free baking powder

- 2 tsp Cinnamon

- 1/4 tsp Sea salt (optional)

- 6 tbsp Butter (softened; can use coconut oil for dairy-free, but flavor and texture will be different)

- 1/2 cup Allulose

- 1/2 tsp Xanthan gum (optional, for more structure)

- 4 large Egg

- 1/4 cup Unsweetened almond milk

- 2 tsp Banana extract

- Wholesome Yum Keto Sweeteners

Instructions

• Preheat the oven to 350 degrees F. Line a 9x5 in (23x13 cm) loaf pan with parchment paper, so that the paper hangs over two opposite sides (for easy removal later).

• In a large bowl, mix together the almond flour, coconut flour, baking powder, cinnamon, and sea salt (if using).

• In another large bowl, use a hand mixer to butter and sweetener until fluffy. Beat in the eggs (use the low setting to avoid splashing). Stir in the banana extract and almond milk.

• Pour the dry ingredients into the wet. Beat on low setting until a dough/batter forms.

• Stir in the chopped walnuts.

• Transfer the batter into the lined loaf pan and press evenly to make a smooth top. If desired, sprinkle the top with additional chopped walnuts and press them lightly into the surface.

• Bake for 50-60 minutes, until an inserted toothpick comes out clean.

- Cool completely before removing from the pan and slicing. (The longer you let it sit before slicing, the better it will hold together. The next day is ideal if possible.)

Blueberry Crumb Loaf – Keto/Low Carb/Gluten Free
Ingredients

For the Loaf

- 1 3/4 cups super fine almond flour

- 1/4 cup Oat Fiber (see notes)

- 2/3 cup blueberries

- 3 eggs

- 1/2 cup sour cream

- 1/4 cup heavy cream

- 1/2 cup swerve confectioners

- 2 teaspoons baking powder

- 1 1/2 teaspoons vanilla extract

- zest of 1 lemon

- Pinch of salt

For the Crumb Topping

- 2/3 cup super fine almond flour

- 3 tablespoons walnuts chopped

- 3 tablespoons grass fed butter melted

- 1/4 teaspoon ground cinnamon

- 1/4 cup Brown Swerve

- 1/8 teaspoon ground nutmeg

Instruction

- Preheat oven to 325F.

- Add all the ingredients for the crumb topping to a bowl, except the butter and mix together. Pour in the melted butter and mix until combined, then set aside.

- Add the flour, baking powder, oat fiber and salt to a bowl and whisk together, then set aside.

- Then add all the remaining ingredients, except the blueberries, to a large mixing bowl and mix using a hand mixer for about 30 seconds. Add in the dry ingredients and continue mixing.

- Fold in the blueberries gently, then pour into a 9" x 5" nonstick loaf pan that's been sprayed with nonstick spray (I used coconut oil spray). If your pan isn't nonstick, I would line it with parchment paper. Smooth the top using your spatular and top with the reserved crumb topping.

- Bake for 45-50 minutes or until a toothpick, when inserted, comes out clean.

Keto Lemon Bread With Poppy Seed
Ingredients

- 9.5 ounces (3 cups) of Almond Flour

- ½ teaspoon of Baking Powder

- ½ cup of Sukrin:1 Sweetener

- 2 tablespoons of Poppy Seeds

- 2 Lemons, zest only

- 3 tablespoons of Lemon Juice

- 3 tablespoons of Unsalted Butter, melted

- 6 Eggs

Glaze:

- 1/2 cup of Powdered Erythritol
- 1 tablespoon of Lemon Juice
- 1-2 tablespoons of Water

Instructions

- Preheat oven to 175C/350F.
- In a large mixing bowl, add the almond flour, baking powder, sweetener and poppy seeds. Mix well.
- Add the lemon zest, lemon juice, and butter and mix well.
- Add the eggs and mix until all combined
- Pour the mixture into your lined 9×5 loaf tin.
- Bake in the oven for 45-50 minutes. The loaf is cooked when golden brown and springs back when touched.
- Leave to cool for 20 minutes.

Glaze:

- Add the powdered sweetener and lemon juice to a small mixing bowl.

- Slowly add the water until the mixture has a pouring consistency.

- Drizzle over the cooled loaf, cut into 12 slices and enjoy.

Low Carb Lemon Blueberry Zucchini Bread Recipe With Almond Flour

Ingredients

- 1/2 cup Butter (softened)

- 3/4 cup Erythritol (or any granulated sweetener of choice)

- 3 large Egg

- 1 tbsp Lemon juice

- 1 tbsp Lemon zest (optional)

- 1 tsp Vanilla extract

- 2 cup Blanched almond flour

- 2 tsp Gluten-free baking powder

- 1/4 tsp Sea salt

- 1 1/2 cup Zucchini (grated - see note)

- 1 cup Blueberries

- Lemon Glaze

- 1/4 cup Erythritol (powdered in a food processor; or use any other powdered or liquid sweetener of choice)

- 4 tsp Lemon juice

- Wholesome Yum Keto Sweeteners

Instructions

- Preheat the oven to 325 degrees F (163 degrees C). Line a 9x5 in (23x13 cm) loaf pan with parchment paper. (You can use foil, but grease well.)

- In a large bowl, beat together the butter and erythritol, until fluffy.

- Beat in the eggs, lemon juice, lemon zest (if using), and vanilla extract.

- Beat in the almond flour, baking powder, and sea salt.

- Wrap the grated zucchini in cheesecloth or several layers of sturdy paper towels. Squeeze over the sink to release as much moisture as possible. Stir the grated zucchini into the bowl, and mix well.

- Fold the blueberries into the batter.

- Transfer the batter to the prepared pan. Smooth the top with the back of a spoon, rounding the top slightly. Bake for 60-70 minutes, until an inserted toothpick comes out clean. Cool completely in the pan.

- To make the glaze, run the sweetener through a blender to make it powdered. (Alternatively, you can use a powdered sweetener directly, like Erythritol Confectioner's or Sukrin Melis.) Whisk together the lemon juice and powdered sweetener. Drizzle the glaze over the bread.

Zucchini Coconut Bread

Ingredients

- 3/4 cup coconut flour

- 1/2 cup zucchini (grated and drained)

- 1/4 cup Pecan (chopped)

- 3/4 tbsp baking powder

- 1 tsp vanilla extract

- 1 scoop unflavored protein powder (around 28 - 30g)

- 6 large eggs

- 1/2 cup butter salted

- 1/2 cup So Nourished Erythritol (or less, up to your liking)

- 1/2 teaspoon salt

Instructions

- Preheat your oven to 350°F.

- Rinse the zucchini well with water and use a hand grater to shred it. Salt the grated zucchini in a bowl. Move to a colander to drain any unnecessary liquids. You should obtain about 1/2 cup of drained and shredded zucchini.

- Start making the dry mixture in a bowl. Fold the coconut flour, baking powder, and protein powder with the sweetener. Mix until blended entirely.

- Beat the eggs in a mixer together with vanilla extract and melted butter. Transfer the grated zucchini in and carefully add the dry mixture too. Whisk together until incorporated. Drop the chopped pecan.

- Coat a loaf pan with melted butter. Evenly spread the bread batter into the pan. Place in the oven for 40-45 minutes or until the bread is browned and cooked. Once the surface turns golden, take out from the oven and let sit for 10 minutes before removing from the pan.

• Slice and enjoy.

Low-Carb Lemon Blueberry Bread
Ingredients

• 2 cups almond flour

• 2/3 cup classic monk fruit sweetener (use code "REALBALANCED" for 20% off Lakanto products)

• 1/4 cup coconut flour

• 1 tsp cream of tartar

• 1/2 tsp baking soda

• 1/4 tsp salt

• 6 large eggs

• 2 egg whites (approximately 1/3 cup egg whites)

• 3 tbsp dairy-free mayonnaise

• 1 tbsp lemon extract

• 1/2 tsp pure vanilla extract

- Zest of one large lemon

- 1 cup blueberries, divided (approximately 150 grams)

Instructions

- Preheat oven to 350 degrees and spray 9×5 inch bread pan with non-stick cooking spray or line with parchment paper.

- In a mixing bowl, whisk dry ingredients together.

- To mixing bowl, add eggs, egg whites, mayonnaise, lemon extract, vanilla extract, and lemon zest. Mix with electric mixer until all ingredients are well-combined.

- Stir in 3/4 cup blueberries.

- Transfer dough to prepared bread pan.

- Bake bread for 20 minutes, remove from oven, top dough with remaining blueberries, and return pan to oven.

- Bake bread for 50 minutes.

- Remove from oven and allow bread to cool for 2 hours.

- Carefully remove bread from pan, slice, and enjoy.

Keto Gingerbread Cake
Ingredients

- 1/2 cup Unsalted Butter softened
- 1/2 cup natvia
- 1/2 teaspoon vanilla extract
- 4 ounces Cream Cheese softened
- 1 large Egg
- 1 1/2 cups almond flour
- 1 1/2 teaspoons Baking Powder
- 2 teaspoons Ginger ground
- 1 teaspoons cinnamon ground
- 1/2 teaspoon cloves ground
- 1/2 teaspoon nutmeg ground
- 1 pinch Salt

Frosting

- 4 ounces Cream Cheese softened
- 1 teaspoon vanilla extract
- 1.5 ounces natvia icing mix

- 2 tablespoons walnuts chopped

Instructions

Loaf

- Preheat your oven to 165C/330F.

- Add the butter and Natvia to your stand mixer and beat on medium speed using the whisk attachment.

- Add the vanilla, egg and cream cheese and combine.

- In a mixing bowl, add the remaining loaf ingredients and mix together.

- Gently fold the dry ingredients into the stand mixer.

- Pour the batter into a 9x5in loaf tin, lined with parchment.

- Bake in the oven for 50-55 minutes, until a skewer comes out clean when inserted in the center.

- Allow the loaf to sit in the tin for 15 minutes before removing to a wire cake rack to cool completely.

- Frosting

- In your stand mixer, combine the cream cheese, vanilla and Natvia Icing Mix. Mix on medium speed until smooth.

- Spread over the cooled loaf and top with the chopped walnuts. Cut into 10 slices and enjoy.

Delicious gingerbread loaf
Ingredients

Loaf

- ½ cup of Butter, softened

- ½ cup of Natvia

- ½ teaspoon of Vanilla Extract

- 4 ounces of Cream Cheese, softened

- 1 large Egg

- 1 ½ cup of Almond Flour

- 1 1/2 teaspoons of Baking Powder

- 2 teaspoons of Ginger, ground

- 1 teaspoon of Cinnamon, ground

- ½ teaspoon of Cloves, ground

- ½ teaspoon of Nutmeg, ground

- 1 pinch of Salt

- Ingredients For Keto Gingerbread Frosting

- 4 ounces of Cream Cheese, softened

- 1 teaspoon of Vanilla Extract

- 1.5 ounces of Natvia Icing Mix

- ¼ cup of Walnuts, roughly chopped

Instructions

- Preheat your oven to 165C/330F.

- Add the butter and Natvia to your stand mixer and beat on medium speed using the whisk attachment.

- Add the vanilla, egg and cream cheese and combine.

- In a mixing bowl, add the remaining loaf ingredients and mix together.

- Gently fold the dry ingredients into the stand mixer.

- Pour the batter into a 9x5in loaf tin, lined with parchment.

- Bake in the oven for 50-55 minutes, until a skewer comes out clean when inserted in the center.

- Allow the loaf to sit in the tin for 15 minutes before removing to a wire cake rack to cool completely.

Keto Pumpkin Bread
Ingredients

- 2 large eggs

- 1/2 cup Almond Flour

- 3 tbsp 100% pumpkin puree

- 1/2 tsp Pumpkin Pie Spice

- 1 tbsp erythritol Optional

- 1/4 tsp vanilla extract

- 2 tbsp Butter melted

- 15 Drops Liquid Stevia Can be subbed for other sweeteners

- 1/4 tsp Pink Himalayan Salt

- 3 tbsp walnuts

Instructions:

- Preheat oven to 350 degrees.

- Combine all ingredients other than the walnuts in a bowl. Mix with a hand mixer or using a food processor.

- Add in 2/3 of the walnuts and lightly mix with a spatula.

- Pour the mixture into the mini loaf pans. If you want to use a standard 8 x 4 inch loaf pan, multiply this recipe by 3 times.

- Top with the remaining walnuts. Bake for 30 minutes at 350 degrees.

- Remove from oven and allow to cool for 10 minutes. Enjoy.

Low Carb Flax Bread

Ingredients

- 200 g ground flax seeds

- ½ cup psyllium husk powder

- 1 tablespoon baking powder

- 1 ½ cups soy protein isolate

- ¼ cup granulated Stevia

- 2 teaspoons salt

- 7 large egg whites

- 1 large whole egg

- 3 tablespoons butter

- ¾ cup water

Instructions

- Preheat oven to 350°F.

- Mix psyllium husk, baking powder, protein isolate, sweetener, and salt together.

- In a separate bowl, mix the egg, egg whites, butter, and water together. If you decide to add extracts or syrups, add these here!

- Slowly add wet ingredients to dry ingredients while mixing them.

- Grease bread pan – I use a little bit of butter, but you can use a substitute spray.

- Add all ingredients to the bread pan.

- Bake for 15-20 minutes until set.

Low Carb Focaccia Bread

Ingredients

- 1 cup almond flour
- 1 cup flaxseed meal
- 7 large eggs
- ¼ cup olive oil
- 1 ½ tablespoons baking powder
- 2 teaspoons minced garlic
- 1 teaspoon salt
- 1 teaspoon rosemary
- 1 teaspoon red chili flakes

Instructions

- Preheat your oven to 350F.

- In a large mixing bowl, add your almond flour. I prefer using blanched almond flour because it's less grainy. Although since we're cooking with flax, it won't make the biggest difference. Just the color will change.

• Add your flax seed into the bowl. I prefer to use golden flaxseed, but I didn't have it on hand. If you use golden flaxseed with blanched almond flour, your bread will turn out much whiter than this recipe.

• Add all your spices and baking powder to the mixture.

• Mix all the dry ingredients well, until everything is evenly distributed.

• Add your 2 tsp. Garlic to the mixture.

• Add 2 eggs to get you started. Use a hand mixer to combine the ingredients, adding 2 eggs at a time once they've been mixed in.

• Add your olive oil in and give one last blast with the hand mixer on the highest setting. The more aerated the batter becomes, the more air bubbles can form and the fluffier it becomes. I personally prefer a denser bread.

• Great a 9×9 non-stick baking pan with butter or spray.

• Pour your batter into the baking pan, making sure you spread the dough out with a silicon spatula so it's evenly distributed.

- Bake for 25 minutes at 350F. The bread will rise, and you'll see it take on a golden brown color.

- Let it cool for 10 minutes. Poke a knife around the edges and try to get a little bit of lift on the bread from underneath. At first it might feel stuck, but it's just the vacuum that was created between the greased pan and the bottom of the bread.

- Turn it upside down then let it completely cool on a cooling rack.

- Add whatever toppings/fillings you want!

Lemon & Rosemary Low Carb Shortbread

Ingredients

- 6 tablespoons butter

- 2 cups almond flour

- 1/3 cup granulated Splenda (or other granulated sweetener)

- 1 tablespoon freshly grated lemon zest

- 4 teaspoons fresh squeezed lemon juice

- 1 teaspoon vanilla extract

- 2 teaspoons rosemary*

- ½ teaspoon baking soda

- ½ teaspoon baking powder

Instructions

- Gather all your ingredients together. Ignore the egg I have pictured, I was initially planning to add it to the dough if I had to, but it turned out I didn't.

- In a large mixing bowl, measure out 2 cups of almond flour, 1/2 tsp. baking powder, and 1/2 tsp. baking soda. Mix these together well.

- Add 1/3 cup Splenda, or other granulated sweetener to the mixture.

- Zest your lemon with a microplane until you have 1 Tbsp. lemon zest.

- Juice half of the lemon to get 4 tsp. of lemon juice.

- In the microwave, melt 6 Tbsp. of butter. I took me about 20 seconds to do this. Add vanilla extract to this and mix together.

- Transfer your almond flour and sweetener to a small mixing bowl. Put your butter, lemon zest, lemon juice, and chopped rosemary into the now empty large mixing bowl. Add your almond flour back into the wet mixture slowly, stirring as you go.

- Keep mixing together the dough until all the almond flour is added.

- Wrap the dough tightly in plastic wrap. This will be the shape your cookies will be when they're finished.

- Place the wrapped dough in the freezer for 30 minutes, or until hard.

- Preheat your oven to 350F.

- Remove your dough from the saran wrap, it should look like a log.

- Cut your dough in ~1/2" increments with a sharp knife. If this knife isn't sharp, it will make the dough crumble. If the dough is still crumbling, that means it needs more time in the freezer.

- Get your cookie sheet out. I use these silicon pads which are nonstick and a huge help when baking.

- Grease your baking sheet with SALTED butter. This adds a great hint of flavor to the bottom of the cookies.

- Place your cut cookies onto your baking sheet, you should have about 24 cookies depending on the size.

- Allow them to cook for 15 minutes, or until golden brown.

- Allow the cookies to cool for about 10 minutes. After that you can remove them from your cookie sheet and enjoy!

Low Carb Microwave Hamburger Bun
Ingredients

- 1 large egg
- 1 tablespoon almond flour
- 1 tablespoon psyllium husk powder
- ¼ teaspoon baking powder
- ¼ teaspoon cream of tartar
- 1 tablespoon chicken broth
- 1 tablespoon melted butter

Instructions

- Crack an egg into a mug. Make sure that your mug is wide, unlike the conventional mugs.

- Microwave butter for 10-15 seconds to melt. Once melted, pour over the egg and mix well. You want some aeration to be done, so the eggs should turn a bit lighter in color.

- Add 1 tbsp. Almond Flour, 1 tbsp. Psyllium Husk Powder, 1/4 tsp. Baking Powder, 1/4 tsp. Cream of Tartar, and 1 tbsp. Chicken Broth.

- Mix everything together well until a slightly doughy substance is formed. Make sure you wipe the edges of the cup where excess dough might be stuck. You want to try to make the top uniform.

- Microwave for 60-75 seconds depending on the wattage of your microwave. You will notice that if puffs up quickly – don't worry, it will reduce greatly in size once you take it out. Once out, turn over the mug and lighly tap it against a plate. Cut the bun in half and sauté it in butter.

Bacon Breakfast Bagels
Ingredients

Bagels

- ¾ cup almond flour
- 1 teaspoon xanthan gum
- 1 large egg
- 1 ½ cups mozzarella cheese, grated
- 2 tablespoons cream cheese

Toppings

- 1 tablespoon butter, melted
- Sesame seeds to taste

Fillings

- 2 tablespoons pesto
- 2 tablespoons cream cheese
- 1 cup arugula leaves
- 6 slices cooked bacon, grilled

Instructions

- Preheat oven to 390°F.

- In a bowl mix together the almond flour and xanthan gum. Then add the egg and mix together until well combined. Set aside. It will look like a doughy ball.

- In a pot over a medium-low heat slowly melt the cream cheese and mozzarella together and remove from heat once melted. This can be done in the microwave as well.

- Add your melted cheese mix to the almond flour mix and knead until well combined. The Mozzarella mix will stick together in a bit of a ball but don't worry, persist with it. It will all eventually combine well. It's important to get the Xanthan gum incorporated through the cheese mix. If the dough gets too tough to work, place in microwave for 10-20 seconds to warm and repeat until you have something that resembles a dough.

- Split your dough into 3 pieces and roll into round logs. If you have a donut pan place your logs into the pan. If not, make circles with each log and join together and place on a baking tray. Try to make sure you have nice little circles. The other way to do this is to make a ball and flatten slightly on the baking tray and cut a circle out of the middle if you have a small cookie cutter.

- Melt your butter and brush over the top of your bagels and sprinkle sesame seeds or your topping of choice. The butter should help the seeds stick. Garlic and onion powder or cheese make nice additions if you have them for savory bagels.

- Place bagels in the oven for about 18 minutes. Keep an eye on them. The tops should go golden brown. Take the bagels out of the oven and allow to cool.

- If you like your bagels toasted, cut them in half lengthwise and place back in the oven until slightly golden and toasty. Spread bagel with cream cheese, cover in pesto, add a few arugula leaves and top with your crispy bacon (or your filling of choice.)

Keto Breadsticks
Bread Stick Base

Imgredients

- 2 cups mozzarella cheese, shredded, (8 oz.)

- ¾ cup almond flour

- 1 tablespoon psyllium husk powder

- 3 tablespoons cream cheese
- 1 large egg
- 1 teaspoon baking powder
- Italian Style
- 2 tablespoons Italian seasoning
- 1 teaspoon salt
- 1 teaspoon pepper
- Extra Cheesy
- 1 teaspoon garlic powder
- 1 teaspoon onion powder
- 3 ounces cheddar cheese
- ¼ cup Parmesan cheese
- Cinnamon Sugar
- 3 tablespoons butter
- 6 tablespoons Swerve sweetener
- 2 tablespoons cinnamon

Instructions

- Pre-heat oven to 400F. Mix together egg and cream cheese until slightly combined. Set aside.

- In a bowl, combine all the dry ingredients: almond flour, psyllium husk, and baking powder.

- Measure out the mozzarella cheese and microwave in 20 second intervals. Stir the cheese each time you take it out of the microwave and continue microwaving until sizzling.

- Add the egg, cream cheese, and dry ingredients into the mozzarella cheese and mix together.

- Using your hands, knead the dough together. Once it is combined, set on a silpat.

- Press the dough flat until you have a full baking sheet worth of dough. Transfer the dough to some foil so that you can use a pizza cutter on it. Knives and sharp objects should never be used on a silpat.

- Cut the dough and season per ingredients above.

- Bake 13-15 minutes on top rack until crisp.

- Serve while warm! You can serve the savory breadsticks with some marinara and the sweet breadsticks with some cream cheese buttercream.

Jalapeno Cornbread Mini Loaves
Ingredients

Dry Ingredients

- 1 ½ cups almond flour

- ½ cup golden flaxseed meal

- 2 teaspoons baking powder

- 1 teaspoon salt

Wet Ingredients

- ½ cup sour cream, full fat

- 4 tablespoons butter, melted

- 4 large eggs

- 10 drops liquid stevia

- 1 teaspoon Amoretti sweet corn extract

Add-Ins

- ½ cup sharp cheddar cheese, grated
- 2 fresh jalapenos, seeded and membranes removed*
- 1 finely diced pepper and 1 cut into rings for garnish

Instructions

- Preheat the oven to 375°F degrees. Prepare a mini loaf pan (8 loaves) by spraying with cooking spray or greasing with butter to prevent sticking.
- In a large bowl whisk together the dry ingredients including the almond flour, golden flaxseed meal, baking powder and salt.
- In a separate medium sized bowl whisk together the wet ingredients. Mix the wet and dry ingredients together then fold the diced pepper and grated cheddar cheese into the batter.
- Spoon the batter evenly into the prepared loaf pan. Top each loaf with a pepper ring to garnish.
- Bake for 20-22 minutes or until the loaves start to turn golden brown.

• Cool the loaves in the pan for about 5 minutes and then remove to a wire rack to finish.

90-Second Keto Bread
Ingredients

- 1 large egg
- 1 tablespoon milk
- 1 tablespoon olive oil
- 1 tablespoon coconut flour
- 1 tablespoon almond or hazelnut flour
- 1/4 teaspoon baking powder
- Pinch salt
- Optional add-ins:
- 1/4 cup grated cheese
- 1 tablespoon minced scallions or herbs

Instructions

Whisk the egg, milk, oil, coconut flour, nut flour, baking powder, and salt together in a small bowl. Add the cheese and scallions or herbs, if using, and stir to combine.

Pour into a tall microwave-safe mug and tap the bottom firmly on the counter a few times to force any air bubbles to rise and pop. Microwave on high for 1 minute, 30 seconds.

Invert mug onto a cutting board and let the bread slide out. Cut crosswise into 1/2-inch-thick slices. To toast, heat a teaspoon of oil in a small skillet over medium-high heat until shimmering. Add the slices and toast until golden-brown, about 30 seconds per side.

Made in the USA
Coppell, TX
04 June 2024